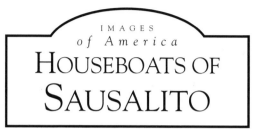

IMAGES
of America
HOUSEBOATS OF
SAUSALITO

Enjoy the story,
Susan Frank

Margaret R. Badger

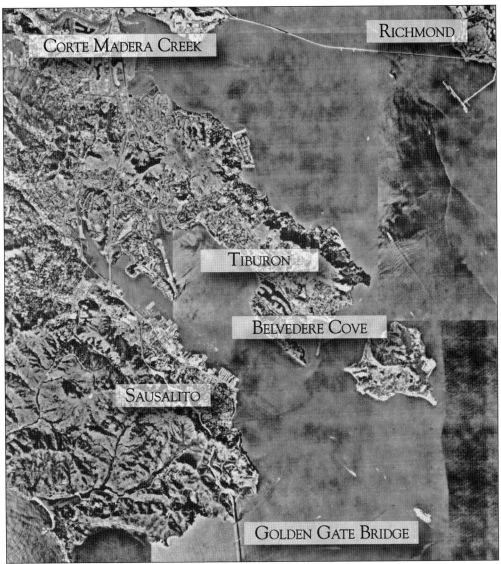

This map of the San Francisco Bay shows the locations of the primary houseboat communities referred to in this book: Belvedere, Sausalito, and Corte Madera Creek. (Courtesy of mytopo.com, locators courtesy of the author.)

ON THE COVER: This is one of the most classic photographs of life on the water in the 1890s in Marin County. It shows the Keil family rowing to their ark in Belvedere Cove to enjoy a day afloat. (Courtesy of Russell and Julie Keil.)

IMAGES
of America

HOUSEBOATS OF
SAUSALITO

Phil Frank

ARCADIA
PUBLISHING

Published by Arcadia Publishing
Charleston SC, Chicago IL, Portsmouth NH, San Francisco CA

Printed in the United States of America

Library of Congress Catalog Card Number: 2007926887

For all general information contact Arcadia Publishing at:
Telephone 843-853-2070
Fax 843-853-0044
E-mail sales@arcadiapublishing.com
For customer service and orders:
Toll-Free 1-888-313-2665

Visit us on the Internet at www.arcadiapublishing.com

My thanks to Susan, Philip, and Stacy
for sharing with me a marvelous life afloat.

EDITOR'S NOTE: Sadly, author Phil Frank passed away during the creation of this book, and its completion was facilitated by his wife, Susan, and the dedicated staff of the Sausalito Historical Society. Phil was an extraordinary man of arts and letters, and his life and remarkable spirit are remembered fondly by many thousands of people in Sausalito, San Francisco, and beyond. Phil left behind an extraordinary body of work; this was to be among his final projects, and all involved are honored to be a part of it.

Author Phil Frank and Pooka strike a jaunty pose aboard the 1910 ark *Ameer* in the mid-1970s. (Courtesy of Susan Frank.)

CONTENTS

ACKNOWLEDGMENTS

There are many people who helped give these thoughts a voice. I am indebted to them for making this book possible. Chronologically, I wish to thank Vicki Nichols and Susan Frank for spearheading the book's organization; Tom Schneider, Barbara Geisler, and Alice Merrill for their design expertise; and Barbara Geisler and Margaret Rose Badger for their editing skills. My special thanks to Alice Rogers for taking all the various pieces of the story and producing the final book. Without the experience and help of a dedicated team of researchers, this story could not have been told.

To Vicki Nichols and Margaret Rose Badger of the Sausalito Historical Society, Piper Berger of the Belvedere-Tiburon Landmarks Society, Alison Moore of the California Historical Society, and Richard and Susan Cunningham of the Larkspur Heritage Preservation Board, I extend my thanks for keeping this and other local histories alive and accessible to all.

Since a story can best be told with images captured through the lens, I wish to thank a group of talented photographers, both known and unknown, who have recorded the essence of this story, including Bruce Forrester, Judyth Greenburgh, Susan Neri, Dona Schweiger, Walter Van Voorhees of the Sausalito Art Source, and Larry White.

There are numerous other individuals and organizations who provided invaluable materials, memories, and images, including Barbara Stein, Neil Davis, Chris Tellis, Miriam Tellis, Laurabell Hawbecker, Robert Flynn, Heidi Foley, Joui Turandot and the Jean Varda project, the Bancroft Library, the Oregon Historical Society, and the City Archives of Vancouver, B.C. I also thank Nick and Susan Cushman for sharing their images of the early days of Corte Madera Creek. Thank you all for enriching this story.

—Phil Frank

INTRODUCTION

Houseboats! Marvelous houseboats! Who among us has not dreamed of a life afloat, waves gently slapping the hull of our floating abode?

One's closest neighbors are not necessarily the folks in the boat next door, whose spring lines are tied to the same piling as yours. Rather, the closest neighbor is often nature, in the form of a curious, territorial seagull planted atop a piling whose beady-eyed stare and raucous call tell you "I was here first!" or the water-frothing schools of herring whose winter mating habits cover your houseboat's hull with fertilized eggs, or the late-night underwater calls of the humming toadfish that send out an above-water drone that keeps many floating homeowners up at night. How about the boisterous sea lion or seal whose begging bark requires you to respond with your own call?

Nature rules on the waterfront, even in the shallow waters of San Francisco Bay. Twice a day the rise and fall of the tides, "nature's crane," raises and lowers each dwelling, even providing a handy lift when transferring a houseboat to a new hull. And life on a houseboat encourages gardens and gardeners. Hordes of potted plants and boxed trees bring forth fresh fruit and vegetables and add their color and aroma to the waterborne.

What further attracts a land dweller to live on a houseboat? Perhaps it is the freedom one feels when afloat or the experience of being untied from the busy crush of life ashore. Perhaps it's the letting go of "convenience" as a measure of quality of life. The task of carrying one's groceries down the dock takes second place to the fun to having a cabin on the water—maximum experience and minimum needs.

The freedom of life afloat does come with responsibilities, but that's the trade-off. Your hull is your security. Whether it's wood, fiberglass, steel, or poured concrete, it must be maintained. Long underwater umbilical cords of water, gas, electricity, telephone, and sewer lines give each boat dweller a sense of security that feels especially good on a stormy, rain-driven day.

Houseboating on San Francisco Bay, especially in Marin waters, has a fascinating and long history. It's my hope that you enjoy reading about it as much as I have in my 30 years of either living aboard the ark *Ameer* with my family or researching the history of life afloat.

—Phil Frank
Sausalito, 2006

This early east view toward the bay shows a father and daughter in front of their ark enjoying a lazy day along the Corte Madera Creek in Larkspur. Other family members enjoy rowing along the creek. The easy access to water and to its many recreational pursuits was always an important part of life aboard the early arks. (Courtesy of the Sausalito Historical Society, Phil Frank Collection.)

One

PRECEDENTS

In the 1880s, the phenomenon of houseboats flourished along the inland waterways of the Pacific Northwest and, to a lesser extent, in San Francisco Bay. Whenever people came to work on the waterfront as boatbuilders or fishermen, riggers, or ship crews, they were often drawn to live in the same area. Their homes were simple in design and construction, without garnish or extensive detail. The roof choices appeared to be limited to peaked or arched. Along the rivers of the Pacific Northwest, owners' wood supplies were stored in the water their workboats floated on. Sidewalks were just enough planks to keep an adult buoyant above the waterline. Some were probably owned by fishing companies, chandlers, and outfitters, and rented or loaned to employees. Humble in origin and design, these first floating neighborhoods were the beginnings of what was eventually to become a waterborne lifestyle. This 1849–1850 watercolor, painted from Rincon Point, is one of the earliest recorded images of San Francisco. The abandoned fleet of square-rigged ships had transported gold seekers from the Isthmus of Panama up to San Francisco. Many of these abandoned craft were quickly converted into storage structures, hotels, and rooming for the newly arrived gold seekers. (Courtesy of the California Historical Society, FN-36482.)

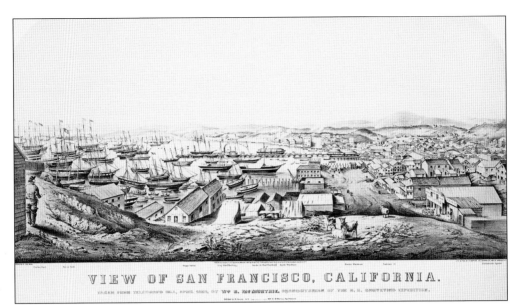

VIEW OF SAN FRANCISCO, CALIFORNIA.

This remarkable 1859 lithograph, drawn by William B. McMurtie of the U.S. Surveying Expedition, captures the San Francisco waterfront from Telegraph Hill. In the foreground, goats graze adjacent to a miner's tent. Below are land-based warehouses, storage sheds, and supply shops, with residences behind. One ship, tied up to the pier, has had its mast removed, and a roof has been added; the others swing on their anchors in response to the tidal current. (Courtesy of the San Francisco Maritime Museum, J. Porter Shaw Library.)

The owners of boats that were destined to become stationary staked out an area for their floating homes in order to claim it as private property. Poles were sunk into the mudflats, and as at the left, the ship was often dismasted and covered by a peaked roof. (Courtesy of the Bancroft Library, University of California, Berkeley.)

Workers at the Canadian Pacific Railroad Shops pause for an 1887 photograph on their houseboat in Vancouver. Many of the area's first houseboats were built by similar workers who created cozy homes for themselves and their families in boatyards. The nameplate on the houseboat, *Bachelors Hall*, is part of the ample roof over these mechanics, foremen, and painters. Their residence is more house than boat because flotation is achieved via logs rather than a hull, as in the San Francisco waters. The canoe in the foreground is identified as coming from a nearby Canadian Indian reserve. (Courtesy of the City Archives of Vancouver, B.C.)

A rare early houseboat photograph shows the style of flotation in the Pacific Northwest. This floating town of houseboats sheltered area waterfront workers around Portland, Oregon, on the Willamette River. Because logging was widespread, logs were readily available for building. Pyramids of logs were lashed together for support and inverted in the deepwater ways. Away from saltwater and its wood-boring teredo worms, the logs would last for years. These communities sprang up along the Willamette River shoreline at the same time that floating homes were evolving in San Francisco and Marin County. (Courtesy of the Oregon Historical Society.)

Two arks have been joined nose-to-tail in this 1890s photograph, taken on a river in the northwest. At the time, this was a common means of creating more living space for houseboaters. The formal pattern of doors, windows, and walkways is consistent with other early images. Note the horizontal flotation log protruding under the front deck. (Courtesy of the Oregon Historical Society.)

This homey scene on the Portland waterfront was captured in the 1890s on the Willamette River, where Canadian Pacific Railroad workers made comfortable homes amid the detritus of the boatyards. (Courtesy of the Oregon Historical Society.)

At the same time that floating communities were flourishing along the riverways of the Pacific Northwest, floating homes could also be found around the inlets and waterways of San Francisco Bay. In this photograph, a string of classic San Francisco Bay arks are moored in a line along the Alameda Estuary around 1900. Level wooden platforms were built along the side of the estuary to provide a resting spot and safe mooring for the flat-bottomed hulls of the arks. Owners paid a monthly moorage fee to tie up their craft. The arks were quite a scenic attraction for visitors. Many postcards of the floating community were created over the years. (Courtesy of the San Francisco Maritime Museum.)

The tide is out on this tethered, World War I–era, settler-type ark in Vallejo. The occupant poses next to his display of potted plants and an American flag. (Courtesy of the Sausalito Historical Society, Phil Frank Collection.)

In contrast to the image above, a fashionable, well-heeled set assembles at the South Bay Yacht Club in Alviso to enjoy some yachting. Tethered to the shore are weekend houseboats for relaxing after the sail. (Courtesy of the Sausalito Historical Society, Phil Frank Collection.)

Two

THE 1880s
A WATERBORNE LIFESTYLE AND ARCHITECTURE EMERGES ON SAN FRANCISCO BAY

Five lasses are making the social rounds on the Belvedere arks in the 1880s. Corinthian Island is in the middle right background with a sprinkling of arks around its base. The little floating structures, the haunts of fishermen and boatbuilders of the 1860s and 1870s, were discovered by San Franciscans hungering for the Victorian pleasures of leisure summer escape. The early houseboats prior to 1900 were called arks because of their ability to float on the tides or rest on the mudflats of the bay, not unlike Noah's Ark. Arks were built in shipyards around San Francisco Bay. The structures were placed atop flat-bottomed scow hulls and built with pocket doors and windows that slid into walls. The roof of each was arched. Gangways went around the structures, with the bow and stern ends being larger and serving as decks. The bow entrance usually had French doors at the center with a single window on either side of the doors. (Courtesy of the Belvedere-Tiburon Landmarks Society Historical Collections, Kimball Collection.)

SAN FRANCISCO, SUNDAY, SEPTEMBER 17, 1899.

WATERS OF BEAUTIFUL BELVEDERE COVE SPARKLED
UNDER GLOWING LIGHTS OF A GLITTERING PAGEANT

Passed Like a Dream of Fairyland Enchantment

Showers of Gold Respond to Touch of Magic Wand

"BEAUTIFUL VENICE, THE BRIDE OF THE SEA."

An article featured in the September 17, 1899, *San Francisco Call* newspaper describes the "Night in Venice" waterborne celebration in Belvedere Cove. (Courtesy of the Belvedere-Tiburon Landmarks Society Historical Collections.)

Belvedere in the 1890s epitomized an ark colony with its annual "Night in Venice" celebration of music, fireworks, and lighted yachts, arks, and homes. The extravaganza was well covered by the newspapers, and the singular event was the talk of area residents and the media for weeks. This is the only known image to capture the magic of the nighttime electrification and fireworks. (Courtesy of the Belvedere-Tiburon Landmarks Society Historical Collections.)

The cover art for the "Night in Venice" program, dated September 16, 1899, which was distributed to early residents, both water- and land-based, around Belvedere Cove, is pictured. (Courtesy of the Belvedere-Tiburon Landmarks Society Historical Collections.)

This marvelous panorama of Belvedere Cove was taken in 1892, capturing nearly 20 arks at their summer anchorage in the cove. Corinthian Island is in the middle of the image, while Tiburon, with its ferry landing, is in the background. The arks were serviced by town merchants

in rowboats, who would take orders for groceries and goods, and later returned with the order and the bill. (Courtesy of the Belvedere-Tiburon Landmarks Society Historical Collections.)

Sausalito's New Town area is captured in this 1909 image that shows seven square-rigged ships waiting at anchor for a shipment of grain to haul to Australia. The owners of the ships, or their representatives, lived in Sausalito. Prior to 1890, Sausalito was heavily influenced by its British residents and was described by visitors as a British colony or outpost. (Courtesy of the Sausalito Historical Society.)

For many years, Corte Madera Creek, located between San Francisco Bay and Ross Landing, annually hosted an ark colony that leased moorings from the State Lands Commission. Hill's Bath and Boathouse, seen in this 1900 view of Corte Madera Creek, served as a community center of sorts for the ark dwellers, providing a place to socialize, take saltwater baths, and pick up one's mail at the Escalle Winery North West Pacific train stop. (Courtesy of the Larkspur Heritage Preservation Board.)

A playful moment is captured in this photograph of several generations of a family aboard their early ark moored along Corte Madera Creek. (Courtesy of the Larkspur Heritage Preservation Board.)

The ark *Alameda* displays full bunting, Japanese lanterns, and patriotic symbols for the Fourth of July festivities on Corte Madera Creek around 1908 in this delightful photograph. (Courtesy of the Sausalito Historical Society, Phil Frank Collection.)

Bathers pose in front of one of the early arks moored for the summer months in Belvedere Lagoon around 1900. (Courtesy of the Belvedere-Tiburon Landmarks Society Historical Collections.)

This early-1880s, box-like ark, the *Woinnebaba*, was part of the Belvedere ark scene. The aft deck served as a social gathering place with lounge chairs and a sun awning. Note the launch side-tied to the ark. Nearly every ark had such a launch for visiting fellow ark dwellers or to go ashore for supplies. (Courtesy of the Belvedere-Tiburon Landmarks Society Historical Collections.)

This is one of the author's favorite images. It captures the mood of life afloat during a narrow period of time in the 1890s. Chinese lanterns, a swinging hammock, and the motion of the changing tides set the idyllic ambiance of houseboat life along Corte Madera Creek. (Courtesy of the Marin County Historical Society.)

Three

MARIN COUNTY WATERS BECOME A FOCUS

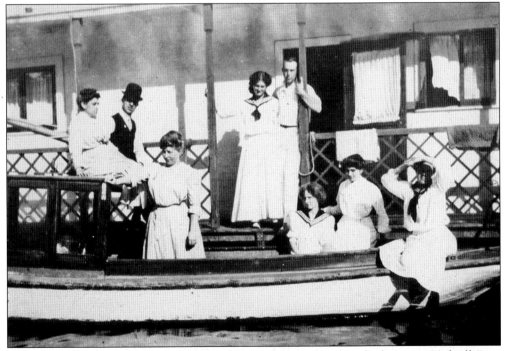

Larkspur, like Sausalito to an extent and Belvedere to an extreme, had its own "Arkville"—a community of floating homes. Its glory days were from the 1880s to 1900. Boardwalks were built that extended from Magnolia Avenue to the creek. The residents of the long line of early houseboats—or, as they preferred, arks—relished the lifestyle of living afloat at high tide and having their floating houses nestle in the marsh grass when the tide had gone out. The line of pre-1900 arks extended for a mile along the western edge of Corte Madera Creek adjacent to a series of boardwalks, portions of which still exist today. The structures were inhabited by the same characters who gravitate toward harbors, fish shanties, and abandoned ferryboats today. One of the highly photogenic features of early arks like *El Bart*, shown here around 1900, is the distinctive cross-bracing on the railings. (Courtesy of the Larkspur Heritage Preservation Board.)

This photograph of Boardwalk No. 2 in Larkspur shows the Escalle vineyards to the rear and an older-style Stars and Stripes above the ark. (Courtesy of the Larkspur Heritage Preservation Board.)

One of the few aerial sots of the arks, this image shows Boardwalk No. 1 and perhaps some of Boardwalk No. 2 in the foreground. To the distant right rear are Wood Island and the "Dirty Harry" railroad trestle over Corte Madera Creek at today's Greenbrae interchange. The hills to the left are now covered by the apartments of Greenbrae, and the salt marsh below them has been filled and covered by the medical/dental buildings along South Eliseo Drive. The meandering dirt road barely visible at rear center later became Sir Francis Drake Boulevard. (Courtesy of the Larkspur Heritage Preservation Board.)

Like a boat, each ark had a name. The *El Bart*, one of the most photographed along the creek, was owned by or was associated with a distillery. Numerous parties and events were hosted on its premises. Some magnesium-flash photographs of the interior were taken in the 1890s. (Courtesy of the Sausalito Historical Society, Phil Frank Collection.)

The detailed woodwork on *El Bart* shows well in this 1895 photograph taken near the site of today's Bon Air Bridge. The Marin General Hospital would eventually be built directly across the creek. (Courtesy of the Sausalito Historical Society, Phil Frank Collection.)

Postmarked 1916, this postcard carries extensive commentary: "The little boy you see on this postal is Willard, and Otto Grundermain in his shirt sleeves and Uncle Geo. Further down. . . . Love, Aunt Tillie." The extensive vineyards at Escalle cover the hills beyond. This shot is interesting for the mud—clearly those arks really float. (Courtesy of the Larkspur Heritage Preservation Board.)

A company outing on *El Bart* is documented in this delightful image, with the gentlemen in their straw hats. The image probably dates to about 1905. (Courtesy of the Sausalito Historical Society, Phil Frank Collection.)

26

The rare magnesium-lit interior image of the *El Bart* from around 1900 bears witness to the attempts to light the interior photographs of the period. (Courtesy of the Sausalito Historical Society, Phil Frank Collection.)

This rare interior shot of the kitchen on *El Bart*, lit with a magnesium flash, gives the viewer a hint of the utilitarian simplicity of the old craft. (Courtesy of the Sausalito Historical Society, Phil Frank collection.)

No image in the ark photographic collections in Belvedere, Sausalito, or Larkspur better captures the architectural design of the early houseboats than this 1910 image taken at Larkspur. The stern awning is ready to be lowered to provide shade. It appears that the rowing skiff has filled with water and sank beneath the stairs. This was likely a frequent occurrence. (Courtesy of the Sausalito Historical Society, Phil Frank Collection.)

With the corporate ark *El Bart* in the right background, a trio of "Arkites" socialize on the boardwalk and enjoy the good life of the ark summer colony in Larkspur in 1912. (Courtesy of the Sausalito Historical Society, Phil Frank Collection.)

Hill's Bathing and Boat House was offshore from the Escalle vineyard just below the Bon Aire Bridge and was reached by an elevated boardwalk over the marsh, which connected Magnolia Avenue with the creek. A popular summertime resort, Hill's Bathing and Bath House was advertised as the warmest salt-water bathing in Central California. This 1910 photograph shows the doors to numerous changing rooms for those wanting to swim in the creek. Also available were boats for rental and a diving float, but guests had to supply their own towels. (Courtesy of the Larkspur Heritage Preservation Board.)

This is an early-1900s photograph of bathing and boating in Corta Madera Creek at Escalle. In the background is the footbridge from Magnolia Avenue over to the Bon Air Hill and Hotel. The bridge apparently had a drawbridge tower accommodating the earlier commercial traffic to Ross Landing. Extensive salt marshes are beyond. This picture must have been taken very close to, if not at, Hill's Bathing and Boat House. (Courtesy of the Larkspur Heritage Preservation Board.)

This is classic Larkspur. Most of the houses shown here on the hillside still exist, with many of them along Magnolia Avenue to the north of today's Lark Theatre. The "E. H. Mitchell S. F." mark in the lower right corner identifies a prolific postcard photographer and supplier. (Courtesy of the Larkspur Heritage Preservation Board.)

Unfortunately, the nameplate above the entry to this peak-roofed ark on Corte Madera Creek is illegible. This ark appears in numerous photographs of the period, always with individuals singing or playing instruments. It was obviously the ark that the minstrels and singers called home. (Courtesy of the Larkspur Heritage Preservation Board.)

A group of what appears to be Sea Scouts poses next to the partly disassembled Green Gray Boardwalk in Marin in the 1950s with a scow schooner as part of the scenery. (Courtesy of the Sausalito Historical Society, Phil Frank Collection.)

By the mid-1960s, the State Lands Commission, which leased waterfront lots to ark owners along Corte Madera Creek, made the radical decision to rescind moorage rights and set a deadline for occupancy. Then they began to destroy the structures with bulldozers, setting the scene for follow-up conflicts in Sausalito during the "Houseboat Wars" of the late 1960s and 1970s. (Courtesy of the Sausalito Historical Society, Phil Frank Collection.)

This rare 1885 Sausalito photograph shows the downtown waterfront on the right and the Old Town waterfront on the left, where an ark can be seen on the ways. (Courtesy of the Sausalito Historical Society.)

A rare photograph of Old Town Sausalito in 1895 captures the stern of the *Spreckles House* at the extreme far left. It was moved from Old Town in Sausalito to Gate 6 at Waldo Point and still resides there. (Courtesy of Sausalito Historical Society.)

Numerous square-rigged hulls lie at anchor in Richardson's Bay in this c. 1910 photograph taken off the New Town area of Sausalito. The town of Sausalito tended to dominate photographic images of Marin County around 1900 because it was the primary port, with shipping, ferries, and cargo coming and going at a regular pace. (Courtesy of the Sausalito Historical Society.)

The Crichton and Arques Shipyard was located at Napa Street between 1914 and 1918, and was active building wooden barges for hauling military weaponry under contract with the U.S. Navy. (Courtesy of the Sausalito Historical Society.)

This is a delightful photograph of the Sausalito waterfront looking toward Belvedere. The photograph shows two early houseboats floating in the middle foreground and railroad tracks in the immediate foreground. The trains arrived in 1875, and the photographer probably arrived around 1900. (Courtesy of the California Historical Society, GN-3277.)

Gussy and Paul Bourdon, longtime Larkspur boardwalk residents aboard their 1900s ark *Ameer*, take to the creek in their freshly varnished powerboat in 1950. The *Ameer* was moored for many years at the site of today's Bon Air Bridge and is presently moored at the South 40 Pier at Sausalito's Waldo Point Harbor. (Courtesy of the Sausalito Historical Society, Phil Frank Collection.)

This 1880 image was taken at Waldo Point in Sausalito and shows a small flat-bottomed scow resting on the tide flat behind the gnarled tree in the foreground. Judging from the visual hints, this could be the first floating structure to drop anchor where today hundreds of houseboats are now moored. (Courtesy of the California Historical Society.)

Beach Road, which joined Belvedere and Corinthian Islands, stretches away from the photographer in this c. 1910 photograph. Smoke chuffs from an outbound steam engine in the distance behind the string of moored arks. The bow of the *Tropic Bird* juts into the center of the image of the middle foreground. (Courtesy of the Belvedere-Tiburon Landmarks Society Historical Collections, Beruguiere Collection.)

Socializing in Belvedere Cove in the 1890s consisted to a great extent of visiting from launch to ark. In this case, 13 stalwart locals dip their oars to visit their neighbors. Beach Road can be seen in the background. One can only imagine the Japanese lanterns and the sound of mandolins and banjos in the summer night air a century ago. (Courtesy of the Belvedere-Tiburon Landmarks Society Historical Collections.)

Creeks and lakes were interconnected in Marin County, allowing boat owners to move from one waterway to another, as pictured here. Because most arks measured 20 to 24 feet wide, there were limits to how many waterways they could enter, but a 3-foot-wide rowboat could traverse every Marin waterway. (Courtesy of the Sausalito Historical Society, Phil Frank Collection.)

Nearly 20 arks cluster next to Belvedere Island in this 1890s snapshot taken from the top of the hill; 10 arks clustered in the cove near Beach Road. All the arks are about "a bottle's throw from each other"—a safe rule of thumb maintained by many harbor owners when anchoring craft in Richardson's Bay around that time. This photograph shows how Belvedere is already becoming built out. (Courtesy of the Belvedere-Tiburon Landmarks Society Historical Collection.)

The cable is taut. The Corinthian Island Bridge is up, and the celebration of opening day of the yachting season officially begins. Now a group of freshly painted sailboats, yachts, skiffs, and arks begins a slow parade to their deeper-water anchorage in Belvedere Cove. Note the ark in the lower left being maneuvered to pass beneath the raised drawbridge. (Courtesy of the Belvedere-Tiburon Landmarks Society Historical Collections.)

The *Idol's Eye* was owned by Nat Goodwin. With its bow almost dipping into the water, the tiny ark is getting a tow to its anchorage. Steam launches were commonly used to move arks to their moorings around 1900. (Courtesy of the Belvedere-Tiburon Landmarks Society Historical Collection.)

The ark *Mikado* was a popular fixture on the Belvedere waterscape. It sports a boat-to-shore launch at its stern and what appears to be a steam launch at its bow for bay cruising. Corinthian Island is to the right, and Beach Road stretches to the left behind the *Mikado*. (Courtesy of the Belvedere-Tiburon Landmarks Society Historical Collection.)

The most infamous of the Belvedere arks in the 1880s was certainly the *Crystal Palace*, which was built and owned by a Mr. McNeil. He had the grand idea of taking four retired, San Francisco horse-drawn cable cars, putting them on a floating platform, and turning it all into an ark that became the focus of an extensive article, "The Arks of Arktown," in the 1899 London magazine *Strand*. (Courtesy of the Belvedere-Tiburon Landmarks Society Historical Collection.)

Another ark featured in "The Arks of Arktown" article in the *Strand* magazine in 1899 was the *Nautilus*. This rare interior shot of three women in full Victorian dress captures the art of leisure in an era long past. (Courtesy of the Belvedere-Tiburon Landmarks Society Historical Collection.)

The arks and the railroad were joined at the hip. The arks, raised on pilings, lined the rail bed of the Northwestern Pacific Railroad (NWPRR), providing year-round housing for the rail workers and, in turn, providing a location to store the arks during the winter season. During the summer, the arks were moored in the deeper-water anchorage of Belvedere Cove. (Courtesy of the Belvedere-Tiburon Landmarks Society Historical Collection.)

A placid 1890s scene of sailboats moored in Belvedere Lagoon greets the viewer. A string of arks—housing for train workers—hugs the distant shoreline as the viewer looks down on the Corinthian Island Bridge. The bridge was raised annually each spring to signal the opening day of the yachting season and its related festivities. (Courtesy of the Belvedere-Tiburon Landmarks Society Historical Collection.)

Mount Tamalpais rises in the distance with Belvedere Island on the left. The NWPRR tracks that served Belvedere and Tiburon from 1884 until 1967 are seen in the foreground and are now the site of the Belvedere-Tiburon Town Hall and Library. The arks on shore were used year-round as worker housing, and the floating arks were used for recreation by weekend and summer visitors. (Courtesy of the Belvedere-Tiburon Landmarks Society Historical Collection.)

In this 1898 photograph, the SS *China* sits in the protected waters of Belvedere Cove, where it is being dismantled. The cabin was removed for preservation and has always been referred to as the "China Cabin." (Courtesy of the Belvedere-Tiburon Landmarks Society Historical Collection.)

The China Cabin, the social saloon removed from the top of the 1866 SS *China*, was eventually restored through the efforts of local preservationists and currently is used for special events at 52 Beach Road in Belvedere. (Courtesy of the Belvedere-Tiburon Landmarks Society Historical Collections.)

Since its restoration, the China Cabin resides on Beach Road in Belvedere, where it is used for special events by the Belvedere-Tiburon Landmarks Society. (Courtesy of the Belvedere-Tiburon Landmarks Society Historical Collections.)

It is the Fourth of July in 1892, and a group of bachelors celebrates aboard their Belvedere ark. The festive air of life afloat explains the quote in the *Sausalito News* of that era: "What Belvedere with its arks could use is a church and a minister." The ark itself appears to be constructed of a ship's cabin moved onto a wooden barge, not unlike the China Cabin described above. (Courtesy of the Belvedere-Tiburon Landmarks Society Historical Collection.)

The massive *Kiora*, also known as the "Polacchi Ark," sits trackside next to the lagoon prior to being moved up the hillside and behind a home. This completely intact ark still dominates the landscape of the hillside at Mar West, where it currently resides. (Courtesy of the Belvedere-Tiburon Landmarks Society Historical Collection.)

Mr. and Mrs. George Wellington's ark, the *Casa del Mar*, was one of the most architecturally interesting of the Belvedere arks, owing to its handsome roofline, shingles, and leaded-glass windows. Through some creative plumbing, running water was provided to the ark. Because of its unique design, any article done about the ark colony always featured the *Casa del Mar*. (Courtesy of the Belvedere-Tiburon Landmarks Society Historical Collection.)

This ark is at its summer anchorage in Belvedere Cove around 1890. Water and hillside summer residences on Belvedere Island combine to form a unique environment of imaginative grandeur. Some of the arks, owned by local residents, were used as additional guest quarters during the popular summer months. (Courtesy of the National Maritime Museum.)

The Trost Brothers house-moving truck, carrying the *Admiral Lewis' Ark* bound for the Maritime Museum, maneuvers the historic houseboat onto a floating barge for its move from Belvedere to the Hyde Street Pier in the mid-1960s. The ark, fully restored, is now a popular part of the pier's collection of historic watercraft. (Courtesy of the Belvedere-Tiburon Landmarks Society Historical Collection.)

A family gathering around 1910 is being held on an ark, which had the distinguishing feature of a ladder going up through the roof. Several generations of local dairy ranching families, including the Texieras, Azevedos, and Bettencourts, have come together for a photograph on the front steps after the ark has been moved to land. (Courtesy of the Belvedere-Tiburon Landmarks Society Historical Collection, gift of Rose Azevedo Cunha.)

Four

CHANGING TIMES
AFLOAT
1906–1940

The San Francisco earthquake and fire of 1906 was the initial trigger for numerous changes on the Marin waterfront. Almost overnight, the early arks became full-time floating homes for the owners who had lost their homes in San Francisco. Between 1910 and 1930, most of the early arks became moored to shore or were raised and placed on pilings to provide shore-side cabins for their owners, or they were sold and turned into housing for fishermen, Italian gardeners, and train workers. Some were moved to the delta area to become hunting and fishing clubs. The last ark was built in Sausalito in 1926. Beginning in 1930, the bridges were built, which left many of the ferryboats without a job or permanent mooring. Many of the area's largest ferries were moved to the Sausalito waterfront, where they were pulled up along the shore, relics of another era waiting for new uses. (Courtesy of the Sausalito Historical Society, Phil Frank Collection.)

Gate Six begins to take shape in this postcard photograph taken about 1952. The structures are mostly old arks on their original or newly acquired hulls. The train tracks that entered the fencing at Gate Six follow the waterline. The photographer climbed Waldo Point to capture the

slowly growing scene. Strawberry Point, at the middle left, shows no structures yet. (Courtesy of the Sausalito Historical Society.)

A classic 1890s ark is shown after its move from a water mooring to land in Sausalito. These arks were cherished by the families who owned them, and the moving of these waterborne homes to land was an event to be celebrated, as in this 1930s photograph. (Courtesy of the Sausalito Historical Society, Phil Frank Collection.)

In the 1930s, the twice-named ark at Gate Six, *Bug-a-boo* and *Pieces-of-Eight*, was purchased by Gene Tansey from Donlon Arques for $10 in gold coin. It was originally moored in Ark Row next to Johnson Street but was moved by Arques to Gate Six. There was no anchor for the ark, but there was an upright piano that supposedly was rolled out the back door and serves as the anchor to this day. (Courtesy of the Sausalito Historical Society, Phil Frank Collection.)

Each of the three Marin towns that incorporated arks or houseboats into its housing mix was used to witnessing arks being moved from one location to another. This tiny ark, owned for many years by printer Gene Tansey, still sits on Sausalito's waterfront at Gate Six. Originally called *Bug-a-boo* in the 1930s when it was located in Ark Row at Johnson Street, it now resides at Gate Six as *Pieces-of-Eight*. (Courtesy of the Sausalito Historical Society, Phil Frank Collection.)

Gene Tansey, a printer in the 1930s, paid $10 in gold coin for his little ark when he bought it from Donlon Arques. First, he secured a spot for it along Ark Row next to Arques's Johnson Street yard, and then prior to World War II, it was relocated to Gate Six. It still sits in the water at Gate Six Road and Bridgeway Boulevard, and floats at high tide. The undeveloped Tiburon Hills are in the background. (Courtesy of the Sausalito Historical Society, Phil Frank Collection.)

The short string of Mono Street arks pose for a going-away photograph around 1950 as the City of Sausalito was beginning to clear its northern waterfront of unwanted structures. Most were burned or torn down. The scene was repeated in 1980 at Napa Street but with occupants still in the structures, city officials watching, and outraged citizens observing. This activity resulted in many changes at city hall. (Courtesy of the Sausalito Historical Society, Phil Frank Collection.)

The unidentified ark in the upper right of this 1890s photograph sports davits and her rowboat off the stern. The smaller ark in the foreground has a unique "over-the-railing" outhouse, a feature that helped to lead to the demise of arks on Richardson's Bay in the late 1930s. (Courtesy of the San Francisco Maritime National Historical Park, John Proctor Collection.)

The ark *Zephyrus*, currently used as a hillside residence on Corinthian Island, is seen in this rare image of an ark under tow to its summer mooring around 1895. (Courtesy of the Belvedere-Tiburon Landmarks Society Historical Collections.)

This four-print contact sheet documents the process of moving the ark *Weona* at the corner of Napa and Caledonia Streets in 1933 in Sausalito. When Bridgeway Boulevard was widened to accommodate extra traffic caused by the new Golden Gate Bridge, the ark had to seek higher ground. (Courtesy of the Sausalito Historical Society, Phil Frank Collection.)

Intricate timbers and cribbing were arranged by the Hanson Brothers house movers in 1933 to create a rail bed on which to move a home from the east side of Water Street over and above the west side of Water Street. The upper floor of the structure was one of the early arks on the Richardson's Bay shoreline. (Courtesy of the Sausalito Historical Society, Phil Frank Collection.)

Named *Weona*, this ark was owned by the Akers family and was situated directly between the Crichton and Arques Shipyard at Napa and Water Streets. The home still exists on the hillside above the old boatyard. (Courtesy of the Sausalito Historical Society, Phil Frank Collection.)

The Akers family gathers for a photograph shortly after their ark, the *Weona* (the upper floor shown behind them), was moved from the east side of Water Street to above the west side of today's Bridgeway Boulevard. In 1933, the county road was still known as Water Street. It was renamed Bridgeway because it would become the primary access to the Golden Gate Bridge, whose construction was just beginning. (Courtesy of the Sausalito Historical Society, Phil Frank Collection.)

A row of classic arks rests on pilings along Wharf Road in Bolinas. Built between 1890 and 1910, these once-floating structures were moved to their present site on the Bolinas Lagoon between

1914 and 1921. The large ark on the left still has its original wooden barge, which was the only form of flotation for these early houseboats. (Courtesy of the Bolinas Museum.)

By the 1920s, nearly all of the water dwellers on their free-floating arks on Corte Madera Creek had become marsh dwellers. They pulled their arks onto the marsh grasses to gain a more secure foundation. The little marsh-dwelling craft seen here was probably photographed from Highway 101 or the NWPRR bridge. (Courtesy of the Sausalito Historical Society, Phil Frank Collection.)

Over time, ark owners built walkways and docks to allow greater access to the creek and the bay. (Courtesy of the Sausalito Historical Society, Phil Frank Collection.)

The Hilton family ark, named *Alice*, is one of 24 arks that were forced to relocate in 1939 from the shore of Belvedere Lagoon to hillside locations in Belvedere. (Courtesy of the Belvedere-Tiburon Landmarks Society Historical Collections, gift of Francis Hilton.)

The *Alice* is presently a residence on Laural Avenue in Belvedere, where it looks fresh and beautifully cared for. (Courtesy of the Belvedere-Tiburon Landmarks Society Historical Collections.)

One of the 1890s arks, the *Pacific Striped Bass Club*, was originally built as a clubhouse and was one of the floating arks moored during the summer months in Belvedere Cove. By 1910, the club had put the ark on pilings along the shore of Corinthian Island. It remained there until the 1950s, when it was moved to the shore of Greenwood Beach Cove in Tiburon. In the 1960s, the ark was once again relocated, this time adjacent to Judge Field in Tiburon, where it was used as a teen center until the 1970s. It was discovered by the author just before its slated last purpose—as a fire training exercise in 1975. In November 1975, Herb Launer rescued the ark and began the long process of restoring the aging structure. Finally, in 1979, the ark was refloated and moved to a new life along Corte Madera Creek in Larkspur. (Courtesy of the Sausalito Historical Society, Phil Frank Collection.)

The *Pacific Striped Bass Club* ark is pictured after it was restored by Herb Launer. It now sits peacefully on its original wooden barge and serves as a residence along Boardwalk No. 1 in Larkspur. (Courtesy of Herb Launer.)

FERRY LANDING, SAUSALITO, CAL.

This *c.* 1890 photograph of downtown Sausalito shows a train arriving at the terminus of the North Pacific Coast Railroad (NPC) tracks and an early houseboat moored off the shore on the left side of the image. Later the NPC became the Northwest Pacific Railroad. (Courtesy of the Sausalito Historical Society.)

In this *c.* 1924 photograph of downtown Sausalito, the terminus of the Northwest Pacific Railroad tracks and the ferryboats waiting to take passengers across the bay to San Francisco and the East Bay are visible. The ferries are, from left to right the *Eureka*, the *Sausalito*, and the *Cazadero*. (Courtesy of the Sausalito Historical Society.)

The ferryboat *City of Seattle*, pictured here behind the *Issaquah*, was constructed in 1888 in Portland, Oregon. Both ferries served on the Rodeo-Vallejo run before being retired to haul Marin ship workers during World War II. (Courtesy of the Tellis family.)

The *City of Seattle* subsequently became a picturesque element of the Tellis family's "Yellow Ferry Harbor," just north of Waldo Point in Sausalito. (Courtesy of the Tellis family.)

The 1879 ferryboat *Vallejo* has received more recognition in retirement than during its years in active ferry service on the Mare Island run. How could this be? Once the ferryboat was taken out of active service, it became a part of the Sausalito houseboat/waterfront scene, with two of the area's most notable individuals sharing the 123-foot side-wheel ferry as their residence. On one side lived Zen philosopher and author Alan Watts, and on the other side lived Greek assemblage artist Jean (Yanko) Varda. (Courtesy of the Sausalito Historical Society.)

The *Vallejo*, a gathering place for the artists, writers, and philosophers of the floating community, became the heart and possibly the soul of the houseboat community of the 1960s and 1970s. (Courtesy of Dona Schweiger.)

The *Charles Van Damme, c.* 1920, could carry 45 automobiles across San Pablo Bay from Point Richmond to Point San Quentin in San Rafael in 30 minutes. (Courtesy of the San Francisco Maritime Museum.)

The *Charles Van Damme, c.* 1945, closes in on the Marin end of her run from Point Richmond to Marin County. This was one of the last ferryboat runs across the bay before bridges were built. (Courtesy of the Sausalito Historical Society.)

Two newly arrived ferries on the Sausalito waterfront in the late 1950s are waiting to be scrapped. The little *Issaquah* was built in 1914 in Seattle, Washington, and went into operation in 1918 on the Rodeo-Vallejo six-minute run. The *City of San Rafael* is tied up just behind it. (Courtesy of the Sausalito Historical Society, photograph by Robert Parkinson.)

What better playground than half junkyard and half boatyard? Gates Five and Six have served for many years as magnets for old boats, vehicles, and an eclectic mix of artists, writers, and families. The children growing up on Richardson's Bay often enjoyed the creative potential of the "gates community" that thrived in the shadow of the ferryboat *Issaquah* on a summer afternoon. (© Bruce Forrester, 2007.)

The ferryboat *Charles Van Damme*, named for a prominent San Francisco businessman, could accommodate three times the number of automobiles as her predecessors. This 1950s photograph shows the ferryboat pulled up along the shore at Gate Six by landowner Donlon Arques. This is the beginning of a new life for the old ferryboat as part of the fledgling "gates community." In the 1960s, the ferryboat was pulled farther up onto the shore, where she was used as a popular restaurant and later as a community center. (Courtesy of the Sausalito Historical Society, Arques Family Archives.)

Five

BRIDGE BUILDING AND WARTIME SHIPYARDS CREATE THE MATERIAL FOR A NEW FLOATING COMMUNITY

This delightful image from the Arques family album captures brothers Donlon (far left) and Bub (far right) with their buddies on the waters of Richardson's Bay, where they spent most of their early years. Donlon Arques described growing up on the water: "I was brought up as a kid on boats. I was broken in like that." Beginning in 1913, the family operated several boatyards on the Sausalito waterfront, the first at Napa Street, then at Johnson Street, and finally at Gates Three, Five, and Six. In later years, Camillo Arques and his son Donlon, Sausalito shipyard owners, acquired a fleet of abandoned ferryboats, grain and vegetable barges, steam schooners, and piledrivers idled by the newly constructed bridges, highways, and trucks. (Courtesy of the Sausalito Historical Society, Arques Family Archives.)

A fleet of new cargo ships was one of America's most pressing needs at the onset of its involvement in World War II. To this end, the U.S. Maritime Commission urgently petitioned W. A. Bechtel and Company to search the San Francisco Bay area for a suitable site for a new shipyard. After an extensive search, the mudflats of Sausalito were deemed most appropriate for a massive shipyard. In March 1942, ground was broken under the name Marinship. Shown in this c. 1945 photograph are the various buildings and facilities of the Sausalito waterfront. The large building in the left foreground was the main shipyard warehouse, which today houses the Army Corp of Engineers Bay Model facility. In the background is the grid pattern of World War II worker housing at Marin City. A small but active village built itself around a market, a barbershop, and a candy store. The plan called for 1,500 family apartments, houses, and resident facilities, including a school, gardens, and a community center. (Courtesy of the Sausalito Historical Society, Charles Walsh Collection.)

A World War I subchaser is one of the watercraft in Don Arques's Gate Three collection, which consisted of every imaginable kind of detritus from the vast Marinship operation. (Courtesy of the Sausalito Historical Society, Arques Family Archives.)

This surplus submarine chaser belonged to one of Donlon Arques's buddies named Brownie. Here it tugs at its Gate Six moorings in the mid-1970s with the *San Rafael* ferryboat in the background. Later the subchaser was moved to Gate Three, where it was part of Arques's personal collection of watercraft. "Brownie," recalled Arques, "was shell-shocked from the war and had a bad temper, and once threw a Chevrolet transmission through the windshield when he suspected a couple of guys of stealing batteries." (Courtesy of the Sausalito Historical Society, Arques Family Archives.)

This rare image of the Sausalito waterfront requires some interpretation. The wooden barges were newly built Arques's boatyard products. During the 1910s and 1920s, these were the primary marine products being built by Camillo Arques at the Crichton and Arques Shipyard at Napa Street and at the Johnson Street boatyards. The barges were used both for commercial hauling of foodstuffs from the delta to San Francisco and for military purposes, per Arques's navy contracts. Beyond the barges, the tethered barge balloon could be anchored to one of three U.S. Army balloon barges, which were later converted into houseboats that today still serve as live-aboard craft in Sausalito. (Courtesy of the Sausalito Historical Society, Arques Family Archives.)

This late-1940s view of the Arques Johnson Street boatyard provides a perfect "Welcome–Get Lost" greeting to all comers. This was a transitional period at the boatyards. Camillo Arques died in the 1940s and willed the yard to Donlon and his brother Bub. Gates Three, Five, and Six similarly came under Donlon's management. At those sites, scrapping operations recycled World War II materials and leftover craft from the ferry systems and the building of bridges. (Courtesy of the Sausalito Historical Society, Arques Family Archives.)

Houseboat Dwellers In West Find They're On Troubled Waters

* * *

A California County Threatens To Demolish Some of Boats; 'Standards Are for Idiots'

By James E. Bylin
Staff Reporter of The Wall Street Journal

SAUSALITO, Calif. — You spot them soon after you cross the Golden Gate from San Francisco and pass through this picturesque community. Old lifeboats, landing craft, submarine chasers, river scows, barges and ferryboats, numbering about 250 in all, stretch for a mile and a half along the shore of an inlet of San Francisco Bay. They're home to hippies, artists, engineers, doctors and lawyers.

On some of the boats, which are mired in mud, the self-styled "working nonconformists" have built $40,000 apartments, designed with imagination and artistry. On others, the dwellers have put up jerry-built shacks. But taken together, the houseboats constitute an artistic community that is a welcome contrast to much of suburbia, proponents say.

Taken together, the place is an eyesore, opponents say.

In the view of some observers, it all shapes up as a battle between the free spirits of a community and the established elders, and the way it looks now it could be a real confrontation. Officials of Marin County have told 36 of the houseboat dwellers that their boats will be demolished unless they are moved. The people won't go, which could mean trouble.

One person who is not too concerned, however, is D.J. Arques, a boat builder who owns many of the underwater lots that the underwater streets run to. Mr. Arques, whom county officials call "the Howard Hughes of Sausalito" because of their difficulty reaching him, says he really doesn't have much control over his underwater lots. Squatters have moved on to his property, he says, "and I don't pay any attention to them." He concedes, however, that a few of them pay rent.

Though he's not as worked up as the residents, Mr. Arques does think the county is wrong in demolishing the boats. Since the submerged streets lead only to his property, he says, the taxpayers' money will be wasted while actually improving his underwater lots. "Where is the public concern?" he asks.

During World War II, Donlon "D. J." Arques was contracted by the U.S. Navy to work at Marinship and at Terminal Island, San Pedro. He was one of the few individuals in Marin with the equipment and the ability to move the heavy material that needed relocation around the yard. In Arques's words, "I built 47 YF ammunition barges, 112 navy personnel boats, two depth barges . . . this was all to clear up Pearl Harbor. The rest of the stuff was navy repairs. . . . I went up and down the coast with trucks—to pick up equipment to build boats with." Arques worked on contract at Marinship until the yard was decommissioned in the mid-1940s. Arques later acquired surplus Marin ships, shipyard land, and equipment, and began renting watercraft to artists and returning World War II soldiers. Ultimately, he would control much of the postwar Marinship property along the Sausalito waterfront. (Courtesy of the Sausalito Historical Society.)

The bear is pictured in his lair. Donlon Arques stands in the Gate Three shop in the mid-1970s. While he was not comfortable being photographed, Arques did allow Bruce Forrester to achieve several insightful portraits. Arques loved his Gate Three shop and the opportunity to work with the old tools that brought him so much pleasure. (© Bruce Forrester, 2007.)

This 1940s aerial photograph of the Arques Johnson Street boatyard shows the flotsam and jetsam that typically occupied Arques's property: semi-floating hulks, craft on the verge of returning to active use or heading for the mudflats beneath them, scow schooners, balloon barges, vegetable barges, tugboats, arks, sailboats—even a World War I submarine chaser (in the upper middle ground). (Courtesy of the Sausalito Historical Society, Arques Family Archives.)

A rare photograph shows Donlon Arques, boatbuilder Sam Anderson, and Arques foreman D. J. in the Gate Three area in the 1970s. After World War II, Arques bought three of the large slipways that were once part of Marinship. He then set up his own yard in the Gate Three area, where he scrapped and repaired boats of many types. Here Arques inspects the reconstruction of his boat, the *Governor M. B. M.* By the 1970s, Gate Three was attracting young people who loved boats as much as Arques did and who were eager to restore one or build their own. (Courtesy of the Sausalito Historical Society, Arques Family Archives.)

This image looks down on the Arques Johnson Street boatyard shortly after World War II, probably from atop the lumber schooner SS *Lassen*. The motley gathering of watercraft in Donlon Arques's collection included tugs, fishing boats, a speedboat and a World War I subchaser. Some of the craft were there to be worked on, while others were there to be scrapped for their recyclable metal. Arques had a group of buddies who occupied the Gate Three shops, lived on the premises, and scrapped the craft that he bought into the harbor. (Courtesy of the Sausalito Historical Society, Arques Family Archives.)

Lindsey Cage, Don Arques's right-hand man at Gate Three, stands at the far right of this photograph of the top of a wooden barge. The barge was one of a number that George Kappas, a neighboring harbor owner, brought in and purposely sank along Gate Six Road next to the Arques property. The idea was to create a road base. In the late 1970s, a Waldo Point garbage truck fell through the upper deck of the wooden barge at this very spot. It had tipped over on its side, but it was righted by a tow truck and driven away. The author was present to witness the spectacle, in which no one was injured. (Courtesy of the Sausalito Historical Society, Arques Family Archives.)

The peak-roofed Spreckles family boathouse is seen in this view from the lower deck of the *Charles Van Damme* ferryboat. It was floated from Old Town in 1959 up to Gate Six, another addition to Donlon Arques's collection. Because it had a number of apartments for workers who maintained the Spreckles' yacht *Lurline*, it was referred to as the Spreckles Hardware Store. It had a number of water heaters, plumbing fixtures, and kitchen stoves. (Courtesy of the Sausalito Historical Society, Arques Family Archives.)

This late-1950s or early-1960s photograph shows an overview of the building blocks of what would eventually become the Gate Three houseboat neighborhood in the 1960s and 1970s. Many of the original shipyard buildings became work spaces for many of the boatbuilders and maritime trades that were drawn to the area because of its proximity to harbors, suppliers, and affordable housing. (Courtesy of the Sausalito Historical Society.)

The Gate Six arks, c. 1938, are, from left to right, *Pieces-of-Eight* owned by Gene Tansey, the McPherson's *Tuli Queen*, the *Hobart Jackson*, and on the far right, the Abrams' ark. The site served as a mail drop, a train stop for Waldo Point, and a parking area for Gate Six. (Courtesy of the Sausalito Historical Society.)

The ferryboat *Charles Van Damme* is shown here in all of its glory, c. 1961, when it had been moved up onto the shore at Gate Six and was being used as a restaurant. Later it was used as a community center for the growing "gates community." (Courtesy of the Sausalito Historical Society.)

Surprisingly, this early-1960s Polaroid photograph is a rare item. It is one of the few images that show a houseboat under construction during the beginning of the second "bloom" of houseboats at Waldo Point in the mid-1950s. During the 1960s, the scow hull with 2-by-4-inch stud walls was moored next to the ferryboat *Issaquah* at Gate Six. The ferryboat is square and true, as yet not beginning to develop its sag in the middle, which was to become its defining shape during its last years prior to its demolition in the 1980s. The ferryboat *City of San Rafael* can be seen at Gate Five in the far right of the image. (Courtesy of the Sausalito Historical Society, Arques Family Archives.)

Another Polaroid photograph from the 1960s building boom on the Sausalito waterfront shows the clearing away of debris to make room for new building on old barges in the Gate Five area. (Courtesy of the Sausalito Historical Society, Arques Family Archives.)

The SS *Lassen* shortly after its arrival at the Johnson Street boatyard looks trim and fit. Later, in a conflict with the city over keeping the *Lassen* at the boatyard, Donlon Arques said: "We went to court, and we found out the city had no right to [move the *Lassen*]. You have to show a need . . . for the public to use the [underwater] street. I told the city 'you move that boat and I'll sue the hell out of you because you'll ruin my ways, and I have a lot of money in that ways.'" (Courtesy of the Sausalito Historical Society.)

Six

SAUSALITO'S BUDDING ART COLONY TAKES TO THE WATER

The Arques boatyards became havens for sculptors, painters, jewelry makers, and bon vivants in the late 1940s and 1950s. The beats of San Francisco's North Beach came to consider Sausalito their summer home. This classic image from Sausalito's heyday as an art colony captures jeweler Loyola Fourtane and her sculptor husband, Ed Fourtane, on the bow of the lumber schooner SS *Lassen* in its berth at the Arques Johnson Street boatyard. The schooner *Lassen* served as a gathering spot for the art colony in Sausalito for many years. (Courtesy of the Sausalito Historical Society.)

This delightful hand-drawn map by Red Raymond shows two artists in the lower-left-hand corner crossing the NWPRR tracks to visit the artist studios aboard the SS *Lassen*. The lumber schooner lived out its days after World War II at the Arques boatyard at Johnson Street in Sausalito, perfectly illustrating the movement of part of Sausalito's art colony to the waterfront in the late 1940s. (Courtesy of the Sausalito Historical Society.)

This early-1950s photograph shows Loyola Fourtane, a nationally recognized jeweler, in her pilothouse studio on the lumber schooner SS *Lassen*. Located in the Arques Johnson Street boatyard, it also served as her home. Fourtane's work was in great demand in museum shops around the country and in Hollywood movies. (Courtesy of the Sausalito Historical Society, Craig Sharp Collection.)

The *Lassen* was a shallow-draft single-ender designed to haul lumber on the Pacific trade route, with a capacity of 700,000 feet of milled wood. The ship measured 180-by-40 feet. (Courtesy of the Sausalito Historical Society.)

Radio shows, parties, media events, unveilings, and award presentations were a part of the everyday scene around the old lumber schooner. When the press needed a quote or a little film footage, the *Lassen* became the destination. (Courtesy of the Sausalito Historical Society, Bob Lackenbach, and Cal-Pictures.)

Juanita Musson or one of her friends from her *Charles Van Damme* days snapped this Polaroid from the upper deck of the *Charles Van Damme*, capturing the little ferryboat *Issaquah* and a 1929 Ford Model A pickup truck in the foreground. Musson occupied the upper area of the *Charles Van Damme* for her living quarters and used the lower level for her restaurant. Turkeys, chickens, and rabbits roamed freely around Musson's residential area. Free-range pets were a part of her restaurant scene wherever she chose to move it. Over the years, Musson relocated her restaurant to at least five different locations in Northern California. (Courtesy of the Sausalito Historical Society.)

Juanita Musson is pictured with the chef at her restaurant, Juanita's Ark, aboard the ferryboat *Charles Van Damme* in the 1960s. (Courtesy of the Sausalito Historical Society.)

Jean Varda (center, with white hair) and his guests are pictured aboard his sailboat *Sakri* on their way to another one of the waterfront parties hosted by Varda. Guests included such luminaries as poet Allen Ginsberg, "Sausalito Sally" Stanford, and sculptor Sargent Johnson. (Courtesy of the *Marin Independent Journal* and Neil Davis.)

Many are the merry pranksters who have come to Waldo Point to put down short or long roots, but few, if any, could be imagined who put down more winding, entwined roots than Jean (Yanko) Varda. A painter and collage artist of Greek ancestry, Varda lived aboard the 1870s ferryboat *Vallejo*, surrounding himself with dancing girls, swirling fabrics, good wine, food, and parties, and, in the process, taking the entire waterfront along for the ride. The giant ferryboat was shared for years by Varda and Zen philosopher Alan Watts. While one would assume Watts and Varda would be as different as night and day, they actually melded like Varda's oils and had a long and prolific friendship. (Courtesy of Vagadu Varda and the Jean Varda project.)

Jean Varda is shown in his later years with guests enjoying a "gypsy encampment" around 1967 on Strawberry Point to celebrate one of Varda's birthdays. Celebrant and friend Mimi Tellis remembers it as "singing and dancing with everyone dressed in exotic costumes and Varda arriving with great fanfare on his sailboat, the *Sakri*, decorated with pennants and flowers." (Courtesy of the *San Rafael Independent Journal* and Neil Davis.)

This 1970s photograph shows legendary writer and Zen philosopher Alan Watts aboard his home and studio on the ferryboat *Vallejo*. (Courtesy of the Sausalito Historical Society.)

This 1970s photograph shows Jean Varda near the end of his life inside his home and studio, the *Vallejo* ferryboat. Varda brought a larger-than-life Greek energy and legendary parties to the Sausalito waterfront. Today the *Vallejo* survives, preserved and cared for where it has been berthed for 60 years. Varda's fabric collages are enjoyed by the many who own them, and the memories of the Greek lover of color and music, and his Zen friend Alan Watts are held close by the entire houseboat community. (Courtesy of Vagadu Varda and the Jean Varda project.)

The *Vallejo* is a 100-year-old ferryboat that spent most of its life on a routine run between Mare Island and Vallejo. The *Vallejo* was originally purchased by artist Gordon Onslow Ford, who shared his quarters with Varda. (Courtesy of Judyth Greenburgh.)

Shel Silverstein, a legendary cartoonist, author, poet, and songwriter, maintained his houseboat, the *Evil Eye*, as his residence on the Sausalito waterfront. The boat, a World War II balloon barge converted into a houseboat by legendary waterfront artist Chris Roberts in the early 1960s, is still there today. Silverstein's books—*The Giving Tree*, *Where the Sidewalk Ends*, and numerous others, have become classic children's literature. (Courtesy of the *Marin Independent Journal* and Neil Davis.)

This is an interior scene from Larry Moyer's anchored-out art studio. Moyer (right) and neighbor David discuss one of Larry's characteristic waterfront paintings. Rowing to a neighbor's houseboat is an important connection among anchor-outs. (Courtesy of Dona Schweiger.)

This anchored-out art studio was built for longtime waterfront resident Larry Moyer. It provides the perfect creative space, surrounded by water, detached from land, and with floor-to-ceiling windows for maximum light. Access to and from the studio is via rowboats seen tied up to the float in front. (Courtesy of Judyth Greenburgh.)

For many years, Waldo Point was as much a concept as an actual place. For nearly 100 years, starting with the arrival of trains in Sausalito in 1875, Waldo Point was a train stop on the Northwestern Pacific line used primarily by shipyard workers and by students traveling to and from high school classes in Mill Valley. At the same time, it was a mythical settlement of writers, artists, musicians, boatbuilders, and dreamers, and remains so to this day. (© Bruce Forrester, 2007.)

Seven

THE 1960S AND 1970S WITNESS A SURGE OF NEW ARRIVALS

An exodus north from Haight-Ashbury after the Summer of Love and a national focus on Sausalito's floating community caused a major spurt in houseboat building in Sausalito. The "Fat Rat Players" go into their routine in front of the ferryboat *City of San Rafael* at Gate Five. The show included songs, dances, musical accompaniment, and blowing the steam whistle on the old ferry. The "Fat Rat" himself can be seen at the far left behind one of his "hench rats," who is handing out Big Bucks (fake cash) to prospective boat slip leasers. (© Bruce Forrester, 2007.)

This late-1970s photograph is an amazing amalgam of the many elements that made the "gates community" at Waldo Point as much an experience as a place. This photograph captures not only the pater familia, Donlon Arques, in his traditional work shirt in the open doorway of his Gate Three shop, but also members of the Snake Theater. These artists and musicians organized the initial protests against a development plan that would push the low-income small-boat owners out of the harbor to make way for bigger, more expensive craft. At the left of the photograph is T. J. Nelson, Arques's harbormaster, who was in charge of the day-to-day operation of the Arques boatyard. (© Bruce Forrester, 2007.)

Laurabell Hawbecker (standing, far left) and her dancing crew pose at Waldo Point Harbor in the 1980s aboard the *Striper*, one of the few houseboats that was seaworthy. When they performed their dance routines, it was under the banner of the Port Side Theater. The *Striper* is unique in that it is one of the few houseboats at Waldo Point Harbor that is mobile. (Courtesy of Laurabell Hawbecker.)

Chris Hardman of the Snake Theater, which was located for several years at Gate Three, sits for a portrait. The Snake Theater eventually became the Antenna Theater and received international renown. In the 1970s, it focused its productions on Sausalito, the houseboat community, and southern Marin County. (© Bruce Forrester, 2007.)

In the 1970s, theater, music, and dance became a large part of the Sausalito houseboat experience. Here Evie Lewis is teaching a dance class to young houseboat residents on the upper deck of the ferryboat *Charles Van Damme*. (© Bruce Forrester, 2007.)

This photograph of a children's holiday party in the living room of the *Ameer*, the author's houseboat in the late 1970s, shows waterfront Santa Larry Moyer distributing holiday gifts to an enthusiastic gathering of houseboat children. (© Bruce Forrester, 2007.)

Laurabell Hawbecker, clutching her radio, stands out in this photograph of a waterfront gathering in the early 1970s. Her delightful attitude and style, combined with her dance troupe, made her an ever-welcome presence at any gathering in the houseboat community. (© Larry White.)

In this 1970s photograph, younger residents of the houseboat community, Subee and her cousin Caitlin, pay a visit to neighbor Piro Caro, who lived atop the old *San Rafael* ferryboat at Gate Five. Caro, who was one of the elders of the "gates community," was a fascinating storyteller and an expert gardener, who filled the top deck of the *San Rafael* with his plants. He passed away in the mid-1980s. (© Bruce Forrester, 2007.)

Part of the legacy of the early houseboat community was the theatrical and musical events that were an important part of life afloat. These events involved all members of the community and provided opportunities for the youngest members to participate in the life of their neighborhood. (© Bruce Forrester, 2007.)

This 1970s photograph shows a perspective view of the Sausalito houseboat community with

Mount Tamalpais as the backdrop. (© Walter Van Voorhees—Sausalito Art Source.)

The *Spanish Helmet* houseboat of "English Allen" has had a long life in the Sausalito houseboat community. The houseboat is based on a steel lifeboat hull and is decorated with Allen's collections of artifacts from his travels. (© Bruce Forrester, 2007.)

The *Madonna and Child* houseboat, created by Chris Roberts from a salvaged piledriver, dominates this 1970 waterscape at Gate Five. Roberts was as much a sculptor as a carpenter and took delight in building marvelous floating constructions. The *Spanish Helmet* is moored on the far side of the *Madonna*. The ferryboat *Vallejo* is shown in the far right of the photograph. (© Larry White.)

Prior to the County of Marin issuing building ordinances for floating homes in the mid-1970s, boat owners created free-form living spaces. Not untypical is the *Clam*, a converted steel lifeboat hull made into a one-woman houseboat at Gate Six. In the background in this *c.* 1965 photograph is the Tellis family's 1880s *City of Seattle* ferryboat, which still serves as the flagship for the Yellow Ferry Harbor at Gate Six. (© Walter Van Voorhees—Sausalito Art Source.)

This is a 1979 photograph of the interior of the restored 1900s ark *Ameer*, which is still moored at South 40 Pier at Wando Point Harbor as of 2007. The family of Phil and Susan Frank lived aboard the *Ameer* from 1973 to 1985. (Courtesy of the Sausalito Historical Society, Phil Frank Collection.)

Phil Frank, a local cartoonist, historian, and the book's author, is seen in this 1977 photograph with his 1928 Ford Model A, which he and his family drove from Sausalito to Maine and back. (© Bruce Forrester, 2007.)

During Maritime Days each year, a theme was chosen, and boats were gathered and brought to the San Francisco Bay Model, where owners would stay aboard for the three-day event. It was a major public relations event for the waterfront and attracted thousands of visitors. In this 1986 photograph, the *Ameer* is being towed to its berth for the Maritime Days. (Courtesy of the Sausalito Historical Society, Phil Frank Collection.)

In this *c.* 1980 photograph, Stewart Brand stands atop the 1912 tugboat *Mirene*, which he had recently purchased with Ryan Phelan. Brand and Phelan spent the next 10 years restoring the *Mirene* into their home. The tugboat is still moored on the South 40 Pier at Wando Point Harbor at Gate Five of the Sausalito waterfront. (Courtesy of the Sausalito Historical Society, Phil Frank Collection.)

This image of the *Delta Queen* and owner Bob Flynn, taken at the Napa Street Pier in 1979, shows the original cabin structure on top of a crew barge that housed workers in the 1920s. At that time, the barge was towed by a tug to a floating work site, where the men would disembark to their jobs. (Courtesy of Robert Flynn.)

The houseboat *Spicebox* serves as the focus for this photograph, which was the cover of a children's book called *Subee Lives on a Houseboat*. Subee sits on the roof of the converted military boat under her father, Eddie's, watchful eye. The *Spicebox* was moored to the ferryboat *Issaquah* for many years in Sausalito's houseboat community. Many copies of the book are in libraries around the United States. (© Bruce Forrester, 2007.)

A rowing lesson, an important part of living on the water, is underway at Gate Six. Stepping off walkways, falling into the water, and getting soaked are all part of the houseboat experience, so swimming and rowing lessons are essential survival skills for the houseboat community. (© Bruce Forrester, 2007.)

Jim Grabham applies a coat of linseed oil, a good foundation for paint or varnish, to seal the Port Orford cedar of this beautiful handmade rowboat. The children are looking on as work progresses in Ray Speck's workshop. (© Bruce Forrester, 2007.)

Each winter, schools of herring enter San Francisco Bay to lay and fertilize their eggs. Sausalito is a focus of this annual rite. The fish eggs, or roe, are considered a delicacy in Japan. The rest of the fish are turned into cat food. The herring fishery brings much-needed jobs to the houseboat community during the short winter season. (© Bruce Forrester, 2007.)

The 1970s were exciting, hectic years in the Sausalito houseboat community There was conflict over development and the enforcement of county and Bay Conservation and Development Commission (BCDC) regulations. Art and music flourished; many times, music, dance, and protest were combined. (© Bruce Forrester, 2007.)

"The Cardboard Front" was an installation created by Chris Hardman and the Snake Theater in 1977 as land-clearing preparations were being made at Gate Five for houseboat pier development. Hardman and other supporters of the small boats that stood to be eliminated by the pier development sought to represent the families and individuals most affected by the proposed piers at Gates Five and Six. The cutouts were eventually bulldozed. (© Bruce Forrester, 2007.)

Saul Rouda, the filmmaker behind *The Last Free Ride*, finds his little sailboat the focus of a push-pull with sheriff's officers as attempts are made to block the pile driver from beginning construction of the Liberty Dock Pier. (© Bruce Forrester, 2007.)

A dramatic scene from the "Houseboat Wars" unfolds in this December 1977 photograph by Larry White that involved the Marin County Sheriff's Department and houseboat owners over occupancy issues at Gates Five and Six. Tensions rose to the boiling point, arrests were made, and structures were seized or demolished. (© Larry White.)

Early morning dawns through the fog on Richardson's Bay, revealing the legendary dry docks. The arrival of the dry docks signified the era of the "pirate spirit" associated with the houseboat community of the 1960s and 1970s. Many free-spirited evening events were held on the dry docks, which became a symbol of the alternate waterfront lifestyle. (© Walter Van Voorhees—Sausalito Art Source.)

Eight

THE TURN OF ANOTHER CENTURY FINDS CALMER WATERS

This is a quintessential view of an anchor-out resident and his dog Arthur rowing to shore to attend to a day's errands. Every anchor-out resident owns a rowboat to access various tie-up docks on the Sausalito waterfront, and their daily comings and goings are a familiar sight. It took 30 years, but finally, issues related to living on the water in Sausalito are resolved between various official agencies. And while no more boats may be added to the floating community, the lifestyle is healthy and continues to fascinate the many thousands of visitors who flock to Sausalito each year. (Courtesy of Judyth Greenburgh.)

Scott Diamond pauses while working aboard his partially remodeled World War II balloon barge at the Sausalito Yacht Harbor. He is remodeling the barge to become a houseboat and will name it the *D. J. Arques* after his former landlord and friend, Donlon Arques. (Courtesy of Margaret Badger.)

A 1980s houseboat sits atop a salvaged lifeboat hull in Kappas Harbor. Many lifeboat hulls were salvaged and incorporated as the flotation for larger houseboats. As seen in the photograph, the old hull is utilized as ancillary space for the residence. (Courtesy of the Sausalito Historical Society, Phil Frank Collection.)

An old live-aboard trailer is being pushed onto a haphazard wood-and-foam raft from its original moorage along the South 40 Pier in Sausalito. The trailer, home for many years to a family of four, was ultimately hauled out and dismantled. It was replaced with a landing craft set in a cement hull, which still resides on the South 40 Pier. (Courtesy of Susan Neri.)

The *Dr. Hatter* was originally built by houseboat resident Bruce Kemper in 1979 as a solar-powered living space (note the panel on the roof). The rudimentary design incorporated an old lifeboat hull. This tranquil early-morning shot reflects the peace and solitude indicative of the anchor-out lifestyle. The solar panel on the roof provides power for its residents. (Courtesy of Judyth Greenburgh.)

Jim Tichy, who had a scientific and engineering background from Stanford, built his home on a self-made Styrofoam base supported on steel ball net floats (used to float submarine nets in World War II, such as the ones utilized at the Golden Gate Bridge). A concrete barge had to be constructed in the mid-1980s to support the delicate tetrahedron pod. Four triangular planes come to an apex triangle at the top. Tichy built part of his entry in a man-powered aircraft competition in the houseboat. Domestic facilities within the structure were said to be limited. (Courtesy of the Sausalito Historical Society, Phil Frank Collection.)

The photograph reveals the details of the front entrance to the houseboat *Apoplexy*, which was a converted 1943 World War II LCVP (Land Craft for Vehicles and Personnel). It currently resides on the Main Dock at the Waldo Point Harbor in Sausalito. The artwork on the boat's exterior was created by the artist-owners, who have lived there for 30 years. (Courtesy of Dona Schweiger.)

The *TK* floats peacefully on one of the pods of the South 40 Pier. This front-entrance view of the converted landing craft is in the style of an Indian junk. Owner Dana Upton has called this whimsical structure home for the past 25 years. (Courtesy of Judyth Greenburgh.)

The *Dorathea* barge, a 1902 flat-bottomed tugboat that began its life hauling hay down the Sacramento River, is now a beautiful home on Liberty Dock for photographer Michael Venera and his family. Because of wear and tear on the original hull, it was put into a concrete barge in the late 1990s, effectively giving it a new life afloat while maintaining its original integrity. (Courtesy of Judyth Greenburgh.)

The *Train Wreck*, a houseboat built by Keith Emmons in the 1980s as a home for he and his wife, is a structure designed around a Pullman train car. Emmons cut it in half and placed a superstructure between the two halves to create the houseboat's great room. The flotation, a concrete barge engineered to support the vast structure, accommodates the lower floor, which is comprised of bedrooms and other facilities. The houseboat sits at the end of the South 40 Pier and enjoys a commanding view of Mount Tamalpais and the Richardson's Bay waters. (Courtesy of Judyth Greenburgh.)

Owned by the Mendenhall family, this building's unique octagonal design on a concrete foundation was constructed in 1979 by Forbes Kadoo, a legendary waterfront character. The houseboat interior has a self-suspending ceiling engineered without posts. It has long been the home for the harbormaster of Waldo Point Harbor. Kadoo also designed the floating island that was moored off Sausalito in the 1980s. It was rumored that the concept for the island was drawn on a napkin over lunch at a local restaurant. (Courtesy of the Sausalito Historical Society, Phil Frank Collection.)

The Issaquah Dock in Waldo Point Harbor hosts a range of diverse shapes and contours. All the houseboats pictured here were constructed in the 1980s and were moved onto the new Issaquah Dock when Waldo Point Harbor was first developed. Although closely spaced, each boat is tied to piers that keep it stable in rough weather. Access to each boat is by a side or front walkway that connects residents to the main dock. (Courtesy of the Sausalito Historical Society, Phil Frank Collection.)

An elaborately designed houseboat appropriately named the *Taj Majal* sits amid sailboats and motor launches at the Sausalito Yacht Harbor. Originally designed for entertaining and residential use, the houseboat has long been a focal point for visitors to the area. (Courtesy of Judyth Greenburgh.)

Longtime legendary resident Ale Ekstrom poses in front of the Gates Cooperative Office. The Gate Six houseboat area grew out of the remnants of the World War II Marinship yard. In the 1970s, it became the heart of the resistance to the development of a larger houseboat community known as Waldo Point, which was planned for the Sausalito waterfront. Gate Six is currently going through the process of developing its own small boat marina for the future. (Courtesy of Judyth Greenburgh.)

The *Night Heron* combines a World War II lifeboat hull of the kind used on Liberty ships and a structure originally built in the 1960s. It was remodeled by its current owner, local photographer Steve Ehret, to include energy-efficient windows and wind- and solar-energy systems. The owner commutes from *Night Heron*'s mooring to his studio in the Marinship yard by motor launch. (Courtesy of Judyth Greenburgh.)

The former ferry *San Rafael* lorded over the neighborhood of Gates Five and Six, where varied smaller houseboats are clustered around 1970. Although many of the boats needed work, the interiors that residents created within were warm and inviting. The graceful curve of Mount Tamalpais sets the overall aesthetic that was such a magnet to this lifestyle. (© Walter Van Voorhees—Sausalito Art Source.)

One of the many children who live in the Gates Cooperative neighborhood strides home on one of the community's many walkways built from salvaged materials. The neighborhood's children all attend local public or alternative schools. (Courtesy of Judyth Greenburgh.)

The *East Farm* houseboat on the South 40 Pier was designed and rebuilt by local architect Michael Rex and his family in the late 1970s. Originally called *Archangel*, it floated on wooden pontoons encased in fiberglass. The present concrete barge flotation was built in the 1980s by local contractor Ian Moody, who subsequently constructed many barges that would give new life to waterfront boats. The inside was masterfully proportioned, utilizing small spaces around a larger room to create a feeling of openness. At the south end, floor-to-ceiling windows maximized the view and captured the radiant light of the water. (Courtesy of the Sausalito Historical Society, Phil Frank Collection.)

This is a stern-side view of the 1912 converted tugboat *Mirene*, with co-owner Ryan Phelan (right) and her neighbor Vanda Marlow on the aft deck. The owners (Ryan and husband, Stewart Brand) spent 10 years meticulously restoring the old tug to pristine condition and adding an engine, which allows them to take the tug for excursions on and around the bay. (Courtesy of Dona Schweiger.)

This is an interior view of the studio of graphic designer Susan Neri on the *Lone Star*, a World War II LCVP. Originally built by veteran houseboater Bob Carrigg, the interior was completely gutted and reconfigured for the present owner's needs in the late 1990s. Ongoing maintenance includes a haul out of the boat at a local boatyard for a week every five years. This includes the cleaning and repainting of the bottom of the hull to keep it watertight and free of wood-boring torpedo worms. (Courtesy of Susan Neri.)

The unusual shape of the *Owl* houseboat, moored on the South 40 Pier, results from the structure being built around a tall dredge tower. Early houseboat resident Chris Roberts's 1970s design was further embellished to give the impression of an owl when viewed from the front. (Courtesy of Judyth Greenburgh.)

Life afloat is never more sublime than when anchored out on a beautiful day in Richardson's Bay. Surrounded by quiet waters, the *Teepee*, which was originally built in the 1970s, has now been rebuilt, given new flotation, and converted into a totally solar-powered, green living environment. (Courtesy of Judyth Greenburgh.)

A haphazard collection of salvaged materials has been utilized to create the *Tortuga*, which was moored in Richardson's Bay. Probably built in the 1960s, it was handed down to a variety of owners before it sank in 1996. At that time, "English Allen" was living aboard. The community came to his rescue, organizing the building of a barge, pictured above, and, ultimately, the refloating of the *Tortuga*. All of these activities were completed in one weekend with the help of many houseboat residents. (Courtesy of Judyth Greenburgh.)

Along the shore between the main dock and the small boat harbor known as the Gates Cooperative are several historic arks. Pictured here is the *Ark d'Triumphe, which* started life as the early-20th-century *ArkElig.* These arks, originally pulled up onto shore after World War II by Don Arques, provide a historical context for the existing houseboat community. (Courtesy of Dona Schweiger.)

It is sunset, and a local enjoys the simple gifts of life on a small houseboat deck. Proximity to the water, replete with sea mammals and birds, and long hours in the sun are among the many benefits of life afloat. (© Walter Van Voorhees—Sausalito Art Source.)

Life aboard a houseboat brings new challenges to residents. Because of the long and sometimes treacherous piers, delivery of mail is often at a central location. Here the community of mailboxes at Galilee Harbor represents the diversity of residents that live in houseboats. Galilee Harbor is the only permitted, small "working waterfront" neighborhood within the Sausalito city limits. (Courtesy of Judyth Greenburgh.)

Part of living in a waterborne community is the celebration of that lifestyle. Residents of Galilee Harbor host the 2006 Maritime Day gathering for local residents and visitors. Since the 1980s, Maritime Day has celebrated the craft of boatbuilding and the benefits of a waterfront life style. (Courtesy of Judyth Greenburgh.)

The Marin headlands are in the background of this view of the Main Dock looking west toward the land. Docks in a houseboat community serve the same function as streets in land-based neighborhoods. They are a place where neighbors meet, talk, and celebrate together. Instead of lawns, each boat confines its landscaping to planters that adorn each side of the dock. (Courtesy of Judyth Greenburgh.)

Proximity to the water allows houseboat residents to relate easily to waterfowl and other forms of marine life. Life afloat is enriched by the night herons, egrets, great blue herons, gulls, seasonal ducks, and thousands of cormorants that populate Richardson's Bay. (Courtesy of Judyth Greenburgh.)

EPILOGUE: On Sunday, September 16, 2007, four days after author Phil Frank's peaceful passing, friends Ryan Phelan and Stewart Brand put out the word that friends and former neighbors would gather along the South 40 Pier in Waldo Point Harbor on Richardson's Bay to say good-bye and fair winds to Frank. As befits a community that loves a party, they came by foot and by water in skiffs, kayaks, canoes, tugboats, houseboats, and sailboats to honor one of the houseboat community's most beloved residents. Just as the houseboat community had first inspired Frank to research and write the fascinating story of life afloat, the community continues to remind all those who visit that living on the water requires a unique blend of independence, cooperation, and boundless creativity. (© Bruce Forrester, 2007.)

127

ACROSS AMERICA, PEOPLE ARE DISCOVERING SOMETHING WONDERFUL. THEIR HERITAGE.

Arcadia Publishing is the leading local history publisher in the United States. With more than 4,000 titles in print and hundreds of new titles released every year, Arcadia has extensive specialized experience chronicling the history of communities and celebrating America's hidden stories, bringing to life the people, places, and events from the past. To discover the history of other communities across the nation, please visit:

www.arcadiapublishing.com

Customized search tools allow you to find regional history books about the town where you grew up, the cities where your friends and family live, the town where your parents met, or even that retirement spot you've been dreaming about.